© 1996 Geddes & Grosset Ltd

Reprinted 1997

Published by Geddes & Grosset Ltd,
New Lanark, Scotland.

ISBN 1 85534 182 4

Printed and bound in the UK

Opposites

Judy Hamilton
Illustrated by Mimi Everett

Tarantula Books

Some things are like each other.

Some things are the same as each other.

Some things are quite different from each other.

But some things are **opposites**.

Day is the **opposite** of **night**.

Here are some opposites:

A **big** house   A **little** house

A **high** wall   A **low** wall

A **long** pencil

A **short** pencil

A **wide** door

A **narrow** door

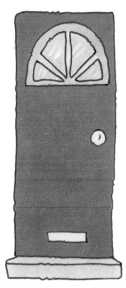

A **full** jug

An **empty** jug

A **large** bag of sweets

A **small** bag of sweets

People, animals and things can be opposites in many different ways.
It might be the way they look:

A **fat** cat

A **thin** cat

A **tall** woman

A **short** woman

It might be the way they sound:
A **loud** bell

A **soft** whisper

It might be the way they feel to touch:
This dog has a **rough** coat,

but this dog's coat is **smooth**.

It might be the way in which they behave:

A **good** boy

A **bad** boy

A **friendly** dog

An **unfriendly** dog

It might be the way in which they move:
This car moves **fast**,

but this car moves **slowly**.

People, animals and things can be opposites because of where they are: This bird is **high up**,

but this worm is **low down**.

This boy is **inside**,

but his sister is **outside**.

This goat is at the **top** of the mountain,

but the goat shed is at the **bottom**.

Different kinds of weather can be **opposite**:
Sunny

is the opposite of **rainy**.

Windy

is the opposite of **calm**.

Foggy

is the opposite of **clear**.

Some feelings are opposites:
Happy

is the opposite of **sad**.

Angry

is the opposite of **pleased**.

Excited

is the opposite of **bored**.

Do you know what these **opposites** are?

Hard

is the opposite of ....?

Light

is the opposite of ....?

Hot

is the opposite of ....?

Dry

is the opposite of .... ?

Forwards

is the opposite of .... ?

When you opened this book, you were **starting** to read it.

Now you are **finishing** the book,
—which is **just the opposite!**

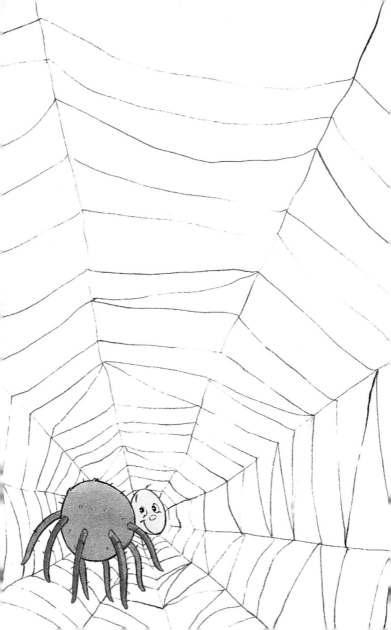